# THE CHARACTER COACH'S PLAYBOOK

*First Edition*

Produced by

*Steve Watson*

*Huey Jiron*

ISBN 978-1-0980-3990-5 (paperback)
ISBN 978-1-0980-3989-9 (digital)

Christian Faith Publishing, Inc.
832 Park Avenue
Meadville, PA 16335
www.christianfaithpublishing.com

Printed in the United States of America

*The Character Coach's Playbook* is dedicated to two groups of people. First of all, to our young people who are in dire need of being challenged and trained in their inner being. Secondly, to the coaches, teachers, and parents who will answer the call of coaching character.

May the character of your soul be strengthened in such a way that it will carry you upward and onward!

You are not alone. *We are*

# About One Team

*One Team* is a movement of athletically minded individuals who desire to serve our local communities by encouraging coaches, families, and professionals to teach their players various principles of attitude and character. As we look at the world that we live in, we recognize that our young people need mentors who are willing to invest in them. The great majority of all athletes statistically will not go beyond high school sports. It is important for us to prepare these young adults for life through the game and not prepare for the game to be their life. Therefore, it is our desire to challenge coaches, parents, and professionals to use their platforms for the purpose of developing the person, as well as the player. We are committed to the character development of all people who will let us into their lives, knowing that our communities will benefit from the strengthening of individual moral character.

# From the Founders

I've been blessed with the opportunity to be a part of the Colorado community since 1979, when I signed a contract to play football for the Denver Broncos. Upon retirement, I started a business partnership, which ended after ten years. It was at this point I was asked by my former coach, Mike Shanahan, if I would like to be a coach for the Denver Broncos in the NFL. My coaching journey for the next ten years took me from the NFL to the college ranks. It was a great opportunity for me to learn from the best and to experience the game at the highest level. A part that I left out, which is very important, was my Pop Warner coaching experience. What I encountered at this level helped me to realize the great void in playing, parenting, and coaching. Huey and I would like to invite coaches, parents, and players to take a deeper look at how we can help develop greater character.

—Steve Watson aka "Blade,"
former NFL player and coach

I have spent over fifty years playing, coaching, scouting, and mentoring within the realm of athletics. Life is like a relay race and I am committed to run to the best of my ability. As a disabled veteran in a wheelchair, there have been many hurdles to overcome. However, our race is short and goes by quickly; therefore, I am passing the baton to you! Take it and run, finish the course set before you. Pass the baton of character to those you influence.

*No excuses; run to win!*

—Al Jiron, Jr., a.k.a "Huey,"
former Major League scout


For 60 years athletics has played a majority role in my life. I began coaching at the age of 16 while I was still playing football, basketball and baseball. I knew quickly that coaching was in my blood and I especially loved coaching softball and baseball at the High school level. Ultimately, I have come to realize that coaching young adults is more about coaching for life and not so much for the big leagues. Over the past decade I have been transformed to a 3D type of coach. I now train the whole person which includes the body, mind and spirit. One of my greatest blessings in life is to be called "coach".

Thomas H. Dillingham, a.k.a "Diller"
Coach—FCA Sponsor

# Contents

# Part 1

# The Approach to Coaching Character

# The Goal of Coaching Character

The goal of coaching character is that you will be strengthened in your inner being in such a way that you will live your life to the fullest without fear of the unknown or the lack of courage to enjoy the adventure. May your eyes be opened to the excitement and blessing of life before you while growing in a humble confidence and recognizing that life is meant to be lived in harmony with yourself and your neighbors. May your heart grow in thankfulness for all that you have been provided with: family and friends, changes and challenges, opportunities and restraints. For it is by all of these and more that you will taste the full flavor of life. May your mind be sound and reasonable, realizing that nobody is guaranteed a tomorrow. Your life here on earth is temporal and fleeting; it is a vapor that is here and then gone. Life is a gift, not something owed to you. Appreciate your time and your journey. Pursue the higher elements of life like your purpose and ultimate destiny without missing some of the temporal pleasures along the way. Being Colorado-strong is encouraging, but being character-strong is foundational! May you grow by grace in the traits of good character and encourage those around you to do the same.

May you live your life.

May you love the life you live.

# Character Development Training

Character makes up who you are. A person with honorable character will be a blessing to family, friends, community, and country. However, these attributes are not easily developed. First, they must be explained, exemplified, and then exhorted to be applied. Once the student of character has a working knowledge of what honorable character is, they are prepared to be tested. The second step in character development is the daily practice. Much like a diamond is developed by great heat and pressure, character will also be developed under the pressures of daily decision making. Many times, you will be tempted to rescue the students from these trying times. Be warned, rescuing does not benefit the student, it only weakens their ability to stand on their own. The best thing you can do for them is to prepare them for life, not protect them from it. It's time to help them grow up!

Even though many want to believe that life is all about having fun, *it's not.* Life will be much more enjoyable when one is able to fulfill their personal responsibilities and face the world with a clear conscience and strong soul. You can play a major role in shaping your community for tomorrow by making a conscious commitment to coach character today.

# Rightly Understanding Sports

Many Americans have recently and wrongly been taught about athletics. They have been told that winning is everything. In the realm of sport, winning is *not* everything. Sport is about participation and playing, growing in knowledge and skill. It's about developing the discipline to be a productive member of a body while decreasing in selfish ambition to be the whole body. Sport is the most enjoyable classroom to learn the greatest lessons of life. Sports are meant to teach us not to quit until the game is over. There are always challenges to work around and within, but no matter what, the game goes on and we keep playing to the best of our ability. That is *victory*. Even though people will differ in levels of ability, the arena of athletics is beneficial for every single person and for the society that participates with a proper perspective and pursuit. Winning is not to be understood as the defeating of others. Being a winner in life is better described as defeating the enemies of a fruitful and joyful journey. These enemies destroy families, communities, and countries. Let us learn to defeat the enemies of selfishness, self-pity, laziness, lawlessness, greed, ignorance, and fear. While maturing in the virtues of confidence, compassion, determination, thankfulness, generosity, wisdom, knowledge, and concern for our neighbors. Let us pursue victory in marriage and parenting, friendships and family, partnerships and professionalism.

All of this can be taught through a proper perspective and approach to sport!

*Sports are all about achieveng your greatest level of personal development, not about developing to be the greatest person. Your only true competition is you. Be the best you that you can be, and you will be a winner in this world.*

# The Coach's Call

When you are called to coach, you are given the opportunity to invest in the lives of every player. With such a great privilege comes a great responsibility. We recognize the heavy workload that all coaches face. Most coaches are bi-vocational with families and other responsibilities. It is difficult enough just trying to teach your players about the rules and skills of the game while also training them in strength and conditioning. That is why *One Team* has put together this simple but effective material. So you can have at your disposal a consistent reminder and guide to assist you in the personal development of your players.

By using *The Character Coach's Playbook*, you will be encouraging your players to practice within themselves the attitudes of a champion. Players who have a good attitude are always the ones who put forth the best effort on the field. Furthermore, people who have the best attitude are people of great character; they go hand in hand.

Here are some benefits for the team that coaches character:

1. Coaching character will strengthen the individual lives of your team.
2. Coaching character will strengthen the unity of your team.

3. Coaching character will strengthen the impact of your team.
4. Coaching character will strengthen the families of your team.
5. Coaching character will strengthen the community of your team.

Make the most of your time with your team. The impact you make today will pay great dividends tomorrow. Finally, always remember coach, they will always remember "coach."

## The Coach's Resolution

- I resolve to use my position to help equip my team for life, as well as sport.
- I resolve to pursue personal growth in my own character so I can be an example.
- I resolve to protect my team from the many deceitful detours that will arise.
- I resolve to encourage the team to be as diligent in the classroom as they are in sport.
- I resolve to be available to the team if anyone needs or desires personal time.
- I resolve to keep my word in regards to discipline even if it costs *Ws*.
- I resolve to treat the team with the same respect that I want them to treat me with.
- I resolve to give my best effort for them before I ask them to give their best effort for me.
- I resolve to give thanks consistently for all the team just like I do for my family.
- I resolve to exhort my team to answer the call of being a young adult and using their platform for the good of others.

_____     _____

(Coach's Signature)                  (Date)

Athletes Arise

Committing to lead your community by example:

- By being friendly to all students.
- By treating your parents, teachers, and coaches with respect.
- By respectfully standing up for those who are being bullied.
- By encouraging others to enjoy their time together at school.
- By watching out for each other's safety.
- By keeping yourself clean from the poison of drugs and alcohol because they affect your mind and the way you think.
- By entertaining yourself with less violence and killing in the games you play and movies you watch.
- By spending time focused on that which is good and honorable.
- By reading or watching movies that are inspirational and make you want to be your best.
- By humbling yourself and serving others.

_____     _____
(Player's Signature)                    (Date)

# Using the Playbook

*I*ntentionally
*M*entoring
*P*layers
*A*bout
*C*haracter
*T*raits

The CCP is designed to be used with a weekly emphasis. Every week, you will have a new characteristic to focus on. At the beginning of the week, take time to explain the meaning and description, along with the quote. It is important to get all the coaches to buy in and commit themselves to grow as people of character. Let the players see these principles personified. Emphasize the attribute of the week in drills and conditioning; write it on the board in the locker room.

We have produced for you *Statements to Coach by*, which are meant to assist you in a very practical way. Make your season about more than just raising up quality players; make it about raising up quality people! Always remember coach, they will always remember "Coach."

# Part 2

# The Attributes for Coaching Character

# Respect

*I*ntentionally
*M*entoring
*P*layers
*A*bout
*C*haracter
*T*raits

*Definition*: Recognizing the value of another person.

*Description*: Respect realizes the intrinsic and external worth of a fellow human. Even if we are competitors or support different opinions, respect allows us to live socially without being enemies. Every human life is valuable.

*Great Quote*: "We must learn to live together as brothers or perish together as fools" (Martin Luther King, Jr.).

*Application*: Think about practical ways you can show respect to your parents, coaches, teammates, and friends this week.

*Words of Wisdom*: Respect all people, love the brotherhood, honor the leaders over you.

*A basic respect is owed to all. An elevated respect is earned by some.*

*Being respectful doesn't mean you have to be a wimp. Hit hard and play hard, but afterwards don't taunt or flaunt.*

# Commitment

*I*ntentionally
*M*entoring
*P*layers
*A*bout
*C*haracter
*T*raits

*Definition*: The quality of being dedicated to a cause.

*Description*: This quality of dedication is that which drives us to continue in the face of difficulty. We will be tempted to quit in the pursuit of our goals because it isn't quick or easy. Commitment preaches to ourselves to press on because the value of what we pursue is worth it: in sports, family, education or anything else we commit ourselves to.

*Great Quote*: "There are only two options regarding commitment. You're either in or out. There's no such thing as life in-between." (Pat Riley, Hall of Fame basketball coach).

*Application*: Make a list of five goals that you are committed to. One in athletics, one in relationship, one in academics, one in community, and one in personal growth.

*Commitment finishes the race because it's motivated by personal pride, the pleasure of pursuit, the pressure of perseverance, and a passion for procurement.*

# Patience

*I*ntentionally
*Me*ntoring
*P*layers
*A*bout
*Ch*aracter
*T*raits

*Definition*: The attitude of being willing to wait so to achieve a desired outcome.

*Description*: Patience is the ability to control one's self for the long haul. It carries the idea of having a long fuse, especially with people. This characteristic is seldom developed but greatly rewarded. True greatness is birthed from longevity and longevity from patience.

*Great Quote*: "Patience is not only an asset for players it is also what coaching and being a sport parent is all about" (Mike Edger, journalist).

*Application*: Write down three areas in which you are struggling with patience. Why are these things worth waiting for?
    Examples: Waiting to consummate a relationship. Waiting for others to develop maturity. Waiting for parents to understand your perspective.

*Even though patience is willing to wait for a desired outcome, it does not wait to prepare for that outcome.*

*Patience involves the willingness to wait. However, patience is not laziness masquerading as virtue.*

*Patience will actively move forward toward a desired outcome while waiting for a chance to prove itself.*

# Preparedness

*I*ntentionally
*M*entoring
*P*layers
*A*bout
*C*haracter
*T*raits

*Definition*: The act of making something ready for ultimate use.

*Description*: The quality within one's own thinking that causes them to recognize their own inability to accomplish a task without further training, teaching, or consideration. Because of this reasoning, a person will continue to become sharper in knowledge and skill.

*Great Quote*: "There are no secrets to success. It is the result of preparation, hard work, and learning from your failure" (General Colin Powell).

*Application*: Write down a task that you are preparing for this week. Then ask yourself, "What am I doing to prepare?"

*Being prepared to compete involves preparation of the body, mind, and heart.*

*One of my greatest concerns is that opportunity will knock on our door, and we will not be prepared to open it.*

# Competitive

*I*ntentionally
*M*entoring
*P*layers
*A*bout
*C*haracter
*T*raits

*Definition*: One who strives or works hard to receive a prize, reward, or position.

*Description*: The quality of one whose want and willingness are combined. Their desire to achieve and commitment to be their best becomes unified within the guidelines of the game or event they have taken on.

*Great Quote*: "When the game is over, I just want to look at myself in the mirror, win or lose, and know I have given it everything I had." (Joe Montana, Hall of Fame quarterback).

*Application*: List some of your desires that you want to achieve. Then ask yourself, are you willing to pay the price to achieve it?

*To be competitive doesn't mean that you always want to win. Being competitive means that you are always willing to pay the price to win.*

# Submissive

*I*ntentionally
*M*entoring
*P*layers
*A*bout
*C*haracter
*T*raits

*Definition*: Willing to place one's self under the leadership or guidance of another.

*Description*: The quality of being a teachable and faithful follower. Not everyone is to lead at all times, that is chaos. But when players, workers, and family members fall into line, we see them march forward in unison. This quality has nothing to do with your essence as a person but is related to your function as a team member.

*Great Quote*: "Above all else, we must learn how to bring our wills into submission and obedience…, on a practical, daily, hour-by-hour basis" (Jerry Bridges, author).

*Application*: List some relationships where you should be submissive, at home, at school, in society, and in sport.

*A submissive player is a real teammate. They follow the leadership of the coach by fulfilling their personal responsibilities as a position player.*

# Servanthood

*I*ntentionally
*M*entoring
*P*layers
*A*bout
*C*haracter
*T*raits

*Definition*: A person who fulfills the role of a helper.

*Description*: The quality of one who is willing to help others. They do not have a problem with menial tasks because they recognize the bigger picture of helping another person.

*Application*: List some people and ways you might serve this week.

*Great Quote*: "Is a servant a dishonorable position or an honorable disposition" (Huey Jiron, former Major League scout)?

*It has usually proven to be true that the greatest heroes are faithful servants. They put the well-being of others ahead of their own pride or desires.*

# Discernment

*I*ntentionally
*M*entoring
*P*layers
*A*bout
*C*haracter
*T*raits

*Definition*: The ability to reason from one's conscience so you can recognize truth from error and right from wrong.

*Description*: This characteristic is vital for solid decision making. It is not led by feelings but by reasoning based on objective principles. For example, don't get in a stranger's car even if you feel safe; stay away. We have witnessed many situations that have led to kidnap and murder, but discernment guides us to be safe because that's the right thing to do.

*Great Quote*: "We need discernment in what we see and what we hear and what we believe" (Charles Swindoll, author).

*Application*: List some ways you might need to exercise discernment.

*Decision making is crucial because your decisions will affect you and others.*

*Discernment is crucial in your decision making.*

# Discipline

*I*ntentionally
*M*entoring
*P*layers
*A*bout
*C*haracter
*T*raits

*Definition*: Training to control and govern one's self to follow a set course of guidelines.

*Description*: The quality of being able to keep yourself on a beneficial course even when it's not easy or comfortable.

*Great Quote*: "Without self-discipline, success is impossible, period" (Coach Lou Holtz).

*Application*: Consider something that you want to accomplish this week. Practice keeping yourself on course until it's finished.

*There is an old saying that says, "Get the log out of your own eye before you tell someone about the twig in theirs." What that basically means is that we should learn to govern our own lives before we try to govern other people's lives. Learn personal discipline!*

# Humility

*I*ntentionally
*M*entoring
*P*layers
*A*bout
*C*haracter
*T*raits

*Definition*: The quality of seeing yourself in essence as being no better or no more important than others.

*Description*: In a very practical sense, humility is that characteristic which keeps one from believing that they are superior to other people. Humility sees people as equal in essence and value while being different in ability, skills, talent, and even function.

*Great Quote*: "Discipline and diligence are up there on the list, but one of the most important qualities of many really successful people is humility. If you have a degree of humility about you, you have the ability to take advice, to be coachable, teachable. A humble person never stops learning" (Todd Blackledge, NFL quarterback).

*Application*: Take time to be alone and ask yourself these serious questions. Do you think that you are superior in the makeup of your being than all other people? Do you think that all people are created equal in essence and value?

*It's hard to humiliate a truly humble person; they don't allow themselves to be exalted in their own heart.*

# Teammate

*I*ntentionally
*M*entoring
*P*layers
*A*bout
*C*haracter
*T*raits

*Definition*: A fellow participant working together for a common goal.

*Description*: The characteristic of a teammate is one who gives their best effort to fulfill their own responsibility to the team while encouraging and relinquishing the responsibility of others unto those fellow participants.

*Great Quote*: "I get asked a lot about my legacy. For me, it's being a good teammate, having the respect of my teammates, having the respect of the coaches and players. That's important to me" (Peyton Manning, NFL quarterback).

*Application*: Focus this week on being a good teammate. Work hard at your job while encouraging others to do the same.

*One of the greatest joys of athletics is the comradery of being teammates. A common battle to achieve a common goal builds an uncommon bond.*

# Thankfulness

*I*ntentionally
*M*entoring
*P*layers
*A*bout
*C*haracter
*T*raits

*Definition*: The quality of honest relief and pleasure for what one has without regard for what one doesn't have.

*Description*: The ability to practice a personal inventory of benefits, blessings, and opportunities on a consistent basis. This practice reminds us of all we have and helps develop a greater concern for those less fortunate.

*Great Quote*: Cultivate the habit of being grateful for every good thing that comes to you, and to give thanks continuously. And because all things have contributed to your advancement, you should include all things in your gratitude" (Ralph Waldo Emerson, author).

*Application*: Take some time alone and write down what you have in material things, family, friends, health, education, and opportunities before you. Then consider all that you have been given in your past.

*An accurate measurement of maturity is when a person attains a cognitive recognition that nobody owes them anything. Everything they have, including friends, family, education, training, jobs, and opportunities are all blessings to be thankful for. Even your daily bread and breath!*

# Perseverance

*I*ntentionally
*M*entoring
*P*layers
*A*bout
*C*haracter
*T*raits

*Definition*: The continued effort to do or achieve something despite difficulties, failure, or opposition.

*Description*: The root of this word literally means "to remain under." It is used to speak of when one is under difficult circumstances. The person who perseveres is willing to pay the price to achieve a desired goal.

*Great Quote*: "Football is like life—it requires perseverance, self-denial, hard work, sacrifice, dedication and respect for authority" (Vince Lombardi, Hall of Fame coach).

*Application*: Consider what areas of your life that you are considering quitting. If you persevere to the end, will it benefit you in the future?

*A great illustration of persevering is the picture of a long-distance runner. The first mile is the hardest, and you think that you can't do it. But as you keep your stride and breathing in rhythm you get your second wind, your body arises to the occasion, and now the competition is on.*

# Sportsmanship

*I*ntentionally
*M*entoring
*P*layers
*A*bout
*C*haracter
*T*raits

*Definition*: An aspiration that an activity will be enjoyed for its own sake with consideration for fairness, respect, and a sense of fellowship with teammates and competitors.

*Description*: The characteristic that makes participation in any endeavor or competition enjoyable. Conducting oneself in such a manner ensures that whether you win or lose, succeed or fail, it was still an enjoyable experience.

*Great Quote*: "A lot of young players really don't know much about the history of the game and a lot of them are missing out on what the game is all about. Especially the whole concept of sportsmanship and teamwork" (Kareem Abdul-Jabbar, Hall of Fame basketball player).

*Application*: Ask three teammates and two opponents if they see you as a good sport. Ask them to be brutally honest.

*A true sportsman finds great joy in playing the game. To participate with others within the rules and objectives is enjoyable in and of itself. After giving their best effort, sportsmen would rather lose than not play at all.*

# Loyalty

*I*ntentionally
*M*entoring
*P*layers
*A*bout
*C*haracter
*T*raits

*Definition:* A strong devotion or allegiance to people, principles, or the pursuit of a cause.

*Description*: The quality of being unwavering in your commitment. It carries the idea of having a single-minded focus. And it flows from a love for and belief in the people, principles, or pursuit that you will be loyal to.

*Great Quote:* "When you're part of a team, you stand up for your teammates. Your loyalty is to them. You protect them through good and bad, because they'd do the same for you" (Yogi Berra, New York Yankees).

*Application:* Take time to ask one of your teammates if they think you are a loyal person. Do you think you are loyal?

*A loyal person will prove to be a champion at that which really matters. A champion at providing, protecting, parenting, and partnering. Loyalty pays well!*

# Integrity

*I*ntentionally
*M*entoring
*P*layers
*A*bout
*C*haracter
*T*raits

*Definition*: The quality of being honest and having high moral principles.

*Description*: This quality comes from the concept of integration. It is when our words and actions match. The person who professes a belief in certain principles or truths and then lives their life according to those principles or truths; that is a person with integrity. When talk and walk match.

*Great Quote*: "The supreme quality of leadership is unquestionably integrity. Without it, no real success is possible, no matter whether it is on a section gang, a football field, in an army or in an office" (General Dwight D. Eisenhower).

*Application*: Ask yourself, what is it that you truly believe about life and relating to others? Do you act upon your beliefs, or do you act upon others' beliefs?

*Integrity is the opposite of hypocrisy. Hypocrisy pretends to be one thing and is really another. Those with integrity will present themselves as one thing and prove their words true.*

# Forgiveness

*Intentionally*
*Mentoring*
*Players*
*About*
*Character*
*Traits*

*Definition*: The intentional and voluntary process by which a victim undergoes a change in attitude regarding an offense, then lets go of negative emotions, such as anger or vengefulness, with an increased ability to wish the offender well.

*Description*: This quality is the key to unity in all relationships. Every person will, at some time, offend other people and also be offended by other people. The natural response to an offense is anger. Prolonged anger will lead to bitterness, hatred, division, and even murder. Anger must be dealt with early. Dealing with anger is much like dealing with teammates who make mistakes. Realize that we all make mistakes. To dwell on the mistake will only cause more mistakes. To forgive allows you to move on together in one accord.

*Great Quote*: "Forgiveness is not an occasional act, it is a constant attitude" (Dr. Martin Luther King, Jr.).

*Application*: Spend some time alone, asking yourself if there is anyone that you are holding a grudge against. When you find yourself willing to forgive them, let them know.

*Let the one who has never needed forgiveness withhold it,*
*but let all who have needed forgiveness offer it generously.*

# Gentleness

*I*ntentionally
*M*entoring
*P*layers
*A*bout
*C*haracter
*T*raits

*Definition*: Sensitivity of disposition and kindness of behavior founded on strength and prompted by love.

*Description*: Many think this quality is a sign of deficiency in passion and power. However, the root of this word literally means "power under control." The one who possesses this quality is one who has the power and strength to blow up but instead, uses that power and strength to build up, much like a nuclear plant. The power that's out of control is destructive, but that power that's under control is constructive.

*Great Quote*: "Nothing is so strong as gentleness, nothing so gentle as real strength" (St. Francis de Sales).

*Application*: Consider this week a situation where you would respond with anger or aggression. Then consider the benefits of responding with gentleness. Do you see the difference that a gentle attitude can bring?

*An example of gentleness is an offensive lineman. When you are truly strong, you can be kind. The one who wants to be seen as strong tends to bark a lot, like a chihuahua.*

# Sacrificial

*I*ntentionally
*M*entoring
*P*layers
*A*bout
*C*haracter
*T*raits

*Definition*: A joyful willingness to relinquish personal rights and resources for the greater good.

*Description*: The quality where desire, denial, and discipline combine to achieve a higher level of success. When a person's desire is strong enough, they will choose not to use all their rights and/or resources for only personal comforts or pleasure. They will only exercise those that benefit the ultimate goal.

*Great Quote*: "A sacrificial person is readily willing to give up and give out that which is rightfully theirs, so others can share in the benefits" (Huey Jiron, former Major League scout).

*Application*: Think of something that you can give up or give away to help another, then do it.

*One time, a quarterback willingly gave up big dollars (that were rightfully due him) so his team could afford a great running back. The result of that sacrifice was back-to-back Super Bowl championships. True story.*

# Love

*I*ntentionally
*M*entoring
*P*layers
*A*bout
*C*haracter
*T*raits

*Definition*: Joyfully dying to self for the benefit of another.

*Description*: The purest form of love comes from the Greek word *agape*. This love is not motivated by selfishness and is not led by emotion. This love is volitional and undeserved. This love loves just for the sake of loving; it doesn't need to be earned or attracted. Agape loves because that's who we are, and we choose to give of ourselves for the sake of another without expecting anything in return but the joy of loving someone.

*Great Quote*: "Teammates show love after a turnover, not just in the end zone" (Steve Watson, NFL player/coach).

*Application*: Think of a practical way that you can die to your own wants and benefit your family this week.

*Words of Wisdom*: There is no greater love than this, when a man will lay down his life for others.

*Love is not just a feeling within, it is an action lived out. True love is courageous, concerned for others, and continues through difficulty.*

*When many say "I love you," they really mean "I love me and want you because of what you can do for me." That's not love, that's selfishness.*

# Confidence

*I*ntentionally
*M*entoring
*P*layers
*A*bout
*C*haracter
*T*raits

*Definition*: The internal assurance that you are capable of facing the challenge before you.

*Description*: This quality grants a person the freedom to pursue opportunities without the fear of failure. It is developed by hard work and trusting in your talent, training, and teammates. This is *not* boastful arrogance. True confidence runs its race and not its mouth.

*Great Quote*: "Confidence comes from discipline and training" (Robert Kiyosaki, author).

*Application*: Are you growing in confidence as a person? Player? Future professional? Future parent? Serious training builds serious confidence.

*Confidence is that which enables us to put feet to our freedom, a fist to our fears, and our face to the future.*

# Faithful

*I*ntentionally
*M*entoring
*P*layers
*A*bout
*C*haracter
*T*raits

*Definition*: The quality of being honest or reliable to fulfill one's word, pledge, or commitment.

*Description*: The quality of carrying out that which you say you will do for a long duration. If you say you will do it, then do it. If you say you will not do something, then don't do it.

*Great Quote*: "The reward of being 'faithful over a few things' is just the same as being 'faithful over many things'" (Author unknown).

*Application*: Make a commitment this week to perform a task, then do it.

*The greatest statement a person could ever hear is: "Well done my good and faithful son, you have been faithful over a little and now I will place you over much, enter into the joy of your father."*

# Part 3

# The Assistance for Coaching Character

# Statements to Coach by

*Respect*
1. You're all needed.
2. We depend on each other.
3. All of you bring something to the table.

*Commitment*
1. There's no quit in us.
2. Perspiration is the price we pay.
3. How bad do you want it?

*Patience*
1. It takes time to develop.
2. Moving forward one step is still moving forward.
3. Wait on teammates; nobody is left behind.

*Preparedness*
1. We're never as good as we could be.
2. Purposeful practice prepares.
3. Being unprepared is ignorance or laziness, maybe both.

*Competitive*
1. Wanting is not enough.
2. Be willing to go toe to toe.
3. The battle is what we prepared for.

*Submissive*
1. Trust your coaches.
2. Follow your leaders.
3. Function as a unit.

*Servanthood*
1. Help each other.
2. Watch his back.
3. Team cares for team.

*Discernment*
1. Think before you act.
2. Deception is derailment.
3. Follow your head, not your heart.

*Discipline*
1. Learn to control yourself.
2. Stay on course.
3. Continue to push.

*Faithful*
1. Live up to your word.
2. Can we count on you?
3. We're trusting in you.

*Humility*
1. It's not about me, it's about us.
2. Exalt team, not self.
3. Many parts, one body.

*Teammate*
1. Together we can.
2. Fulfill your responsibility.
3. Encourage others to achieve.

*Thankfulness*
1. Appreciate the opportunity before you.
2. Nobody owes you anything.
3. Make the most of today.

*Perseverance*
1. Quitting is not an option.
2. Finish the race you started.
3. Keep going until victory.

*Sportsmanship*
1. Champions are not cheaters.
2. Competitors are partners in the game.
3. Stay within the rules.

*Loyalty*
1. Brotherhood is unwavering.
2. Be devoted to the cause.
3. Keep a single-minded focus.

*Integrity*
1. Walk your talk.
2. Live like you want to be.
3. Practice being your best.

*Forgiveness*
1. Everyone makes mistakes.
2. Anger clouds our thinking.
3. Bitterness divides.

*Gentleness*
1. The strong can control their anger.
2. Strength is not just found in a bench press.
3. Power that builds is invaluable.

*Sacrificial*
1. Are you willing to pay the price?
2. Because you can doesn't mean you should.
3. Lay down your ego.

*Love*
1. Give yourself for the cause.
2. For the sake of the team.
3. Team goals over personal wants.

*Confidence*
1. You are prepared for this.
2. You can do it.
3. You can play with anyone.

# Character Quotes

1. Character is the concrete needed to build a solid life.
2. In good times, you can *act* like you have character; in tough times, everyone will know if you have character.
3. Character is like gold; it must be tested to prove its authenticity.
4. If character lives inside, it will walk outside.
5. The pursuit of character is honorable, the manifestation of character is beautiful, and the qualities of character are eternal.
6. Character is like myrrh, only when the carrier is crushed does the beautiful aroma release.
7. Perfect character: no one has attained it; yet everyone can pursue it.
8. To start pursuing character, it takes a decision. To keep pursuing character, it takes a conviction. To finish pursuing character, it takes transformation.
9. Personal character unifies people, solidifies society, and clarifies priorities.
10. Character development is like marriage: it's perfect in principle but needs patience in practice.
11. Character will flow from our being into our doing so focus on being a person of character.

12. Our need of the day is not better laws but better people. The government cannot legislate morality but character development will.
13. Sports are games and games are for play. Ultimately they don't count. Character is for life. Life is not a game. Ultimately character counts.

# Special Thanks

One Team would like to offer our appreciation to those who helped make this possible:

Tamara Rogers for typing and retyping our manuscripts.

- Kolt Bridges and Russ Morrison for serving as our layout designers.
- Our Leadership Team for their ideas and contributions.
- And especially the ladies that complete our lives, Pam Watson and Lori Jiron.

# Contacts

For more information or to order more books, contact us at:
WEAREONE-TEAM.COM

    For further personal growth:
- Fellowship of Christian Athletes—fca.org
- Lochwood Christian Fellowship—lochwood.church

    *We are One Team.*

# About the Authors

Steve Watson is a resident of Colorado who played professional football for the Denver Broncos. After playing in the Super Bowl and the Pro Bowl, Steve served on the coaching staff of the Broncos. Steve now encourages his community by speaking to athletes, coaches, and parents about growing in personal character. Steve is married to Pam and together have three children and grandchildren. Steve is a graduate of Temple University.

Huey Jiron is a speaker who has traveled the world, proclaiming the message of mentorship through sports. He believes that the greatest classroom is the field of competition. Huey played for the Arkansas Razorbacks before serving in the US Navy. As a disabled veteran, he coached for ten years, then scouted for MLB. He holds two master's degrees. Huey is married to Lori since 1984, and together they have three children and one granddaughter named Autumn.

CPSIA information can be obtained
at www.ICGtesting.com
Printed in the USA
LVHW090030291220
674973LV00006BA/924

9 781098 039905